Contents

Mouse tales

In the past, Quarry Bank was home to hundreds of mice! Look out for

GW00469009

This book contains lots of fun things to do. Why not try your hand at weaving, take the apprentice test or make some mill porridge? (Yuck!)

Then and now

You can compare your life today to the way people used to live at Quarry Bank. Life was so much harder for children then.

I'M CRAIG

I enjoy being outdoors because there's always something surprising to discover, like the fish pass on the river.

FIND OUT MORE ABOUT QUARRY BANK WILDLIFE ON PAGE 20.

How did Quarry Bank get started?

If you were left a fortune, how would you spend it?

That was the big question facing Samuel Greg. He could have bought a fancy mansion and never worked again. He could have held amazing parties for his friends. But Samuel had a very different dream...

He decided to build an enormous cotton mill and fill it with the latest, hi-tech machinery.

Samuel was just 25 when he began to build his mill. He devoted the rest of his life to Quarry Bank.

Portrait of Samuel Greg

A MILL BY A RIVER

When Samuel was looking for somewhere to build his mill he needed a place that was near a river to power his machines and near the Liverpool docks and canals as well. The Bollin valley was the perfect spot. Water from the river drove the massive waterwheel he built which provided power to his mill. Quarry Bank mill was an enormous building, full of noisy, clanking machines to prepare and spin cotton.

Once the mill was built, Samuel needed workers. He built an Apprentice House for the children who came to work at the mill, a home for his family and cottages for his workers.

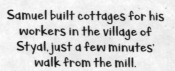

Samuel built cottages for his workers in the village of Styal, just a few minutes' walk from the mill.

A FAMILY HOME

A few years after he opened Quarry Bank mill, Samuel got married. Together, Samuel and Hannah Greg had 13 children! Imagine 12 brothers and sisters! They loved Quarry Bank so much that they built their family home right next door to the mill. They also created a beautiful garden, where the children could play and Samuel could relax after a hard day's work.

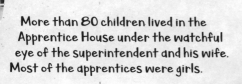

More than 80 children lived in the Apprentice House under the watchful eye of the superintendent and his wife. Most of the apprentices were girls.

Where did the cotton come from?

Huge bales of cotton arrived by ship at the nearby port of Liverpool. The cotton came from plants that grew on plantations in the southern states of America. African slaves worked on the American plantations. Life was very hard for the mill workers, but for the slaves who picked the cotton it was even worse as many plantation owners were very cruel to their slaves.

What kind of jobs did people do at the mill?

All sorts of jobs were needed to keep the mill running smoothly. A few workers spent their day as clerks in the counting house, but most people had to work on the machines. They suffered hours of heat and dust, deafening noise and nasty smells.

Clerks worked in the counting house, writing letters and keeping accounts. They earned more than three times as much as the ordinary mill workers.

MANY ROOMS

The mill was divided into several large rooms, and each room housed machines for different jobs. There were machines for preparing the cotton, spinning the thread, weaving the cloth, and packing it away. A few men ran the water wheel and the largest machines that needed strength, but women were in charge of many more machines. I wonder why?

The weaving shed was one of the noisiest places in Quarry Bank mill.

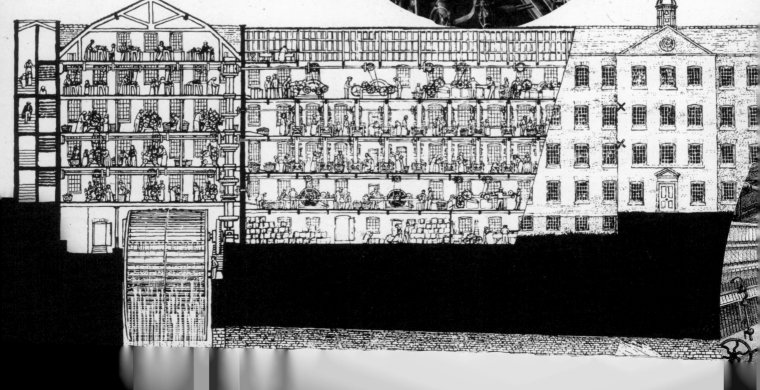

DIFFERENT PAY

Working hours were very long, at least 12 hours a day, but everyone was given different pay, even for doing the same work. Is that fair? In the 1850s, men were paid up to 15 shillings a week (£70 in today's money), women earned around 8 shillings (£36), and children only earned 3 shillings (£14) a week. How much would you pay the men, women and children, if you were Samuel Greg?

Name that job!

Some jobs in the mill had very strange names. Can you match the job name to its description? You could draw a line between them.
(Answers on page 24)

Job title	Description
1 Warping	**A** Brushing and cleaning the raw cotton
2 Carding	**B** Removing full bobbins of thread
3 Drawing	**C** Mending broken threads
4 Piecing	**D** Preparing thread for the looms
5 Doffing	**E** Stretching the cotton fibres

> Which of these jobs do you think sounds the hardest?

JOBS FOR CHILDREN

Children were really useful in the mill. They were small enough to crawl under the machinery, and their fingers were tiny, the perfect size to join threads.
Imagine. For 12 hours a day machines are clanking, spinning and whirring around you. Your job is to crawl under moving machinery to clean the dust out from underneath. You join broken threads, sweep the floors, and carry heavy cans of cotton to different parts of the mill. It is boring, tiring and very dangerous.

> Small children, known as scavengers, would crawl under the machinery.

Kissing the shuttle

To thread the shuttle the worker had to suck the thread through a hole at one end. This is called 'kissing the shuttle'. Sadly, it led to some very nasty diseases of the mouth. Think of all those germs! Yuck!

Who were the apprentices?

Some child workers went home to their family at the end of the day, but others were not so lucky. They were the apprentices who were sent from towns and cities to work at Quarry Bank. Most apprentices came from the workhouse – a place where children went to live if their parents had died or if they were too poor to look after their children.

Workhouses were harsh and scary places, but for many children the workhouse was the only home they knew.

Apprentices signed an indenture when they arrived. This was a contract that made them the property of Samuel Greg and stated they had to work at Quarry Bank for up to nine years. If they left they were breaking the law and would be arrested!

A TERRIFYING JOURNEY

Imagine being nine years old and saying goodbye to everything you had ever known...

You would travel by horse and cart, until you arrived, tired and scared, at the Apprentice House. Then you would be put to bed with another child you had never seen before. Early the next morning you would start your new life as a worker in the huge and frightening mill. No wonder many apprentices cried themselves to sleep and made plans to run away and find their way back home!

The apprentices slept two to a bed, in wooden boxes known as coffin beds.

Be it remembered, it is and between SAMUEL GREG, of Styal, ter, of the one Part, and *Ann Bat*

Morley in the County of Chester as follows: That the said *Ann M* serve the said SAMUEL GREG, in his Co County of Chester, as a just and hones Hours in each of the six working Da Liberty at all other Times ; the Co to be fixed from Time to Time by the Term of *Two* Years *Shillings & Six pence* a Mule or any other said *McGreg shall Put*

And that if the said *Ann* shall absent *himself* from the S in the said working Hours, his Consent first obtained, abate the Wages in a double the said SAMUEL GREG shal discharge the Servant fror Want of Employ.

As Witness their Han *December* 1795

ESTHER'S STORY

Esther Price was born in Liverpool in 1820, and spent at least some of her childhood in the workhouse because her family was so poor. She was 13 years old when she was sent to Quarry Bank, where she soon got into trouble for bad behaviour. When she was 16, Esther ran away, back to Liverpool, with her friend Lucy. They did come back to Quarry Bank, but running away was breaking the law, so they were punished. Esther was kept in a darkened room and fed on gruel (thin porridge) and bread for seven days – the number of days she had been missing.

After that experience, Esther settled down and worked in the mill for many years. She lived in Styal with her husband and children.

Are you big enough to work?

Some apprentices who looked very small might have had to take a test before they started work. Why not try this test for yourself? Stand up straight and put your right arm over your head. Can you touch your left ear with your hand? If you can, that's great! It means you're big enough to start work at the mill.

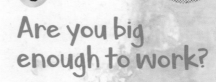

Runaway numbers

In the 30 years between 1815 and 1845, at least 23 apprentices ran away from Quarry Bank. All except four were found and brought back again.

What was life like for an apprentice?

Imagine a working day that started at six in the morning and didn't end until seven o'clock at night. Then think of repeating it six days a week. On top of that, there were jobs in the house and garden, lessons once a week, and long walks to church on Sundays. It's hardly surprising that some apprentices tried to run away!

NASTY START

What's the first thing you do when you wake up? For the apprentices, it was slopping out. This involved emptying the chamber pots that they used as toilets that were kept under their beds. Not a very pleasant way to start the day!

The apprentice boys had to recite times tables and practise handwriting. Their lessons were very boring!

LESSON TIME

Once a week, the apprentices had lessons at the end of their working day. The boys were taught basic reading, writing and arithmetic. The girls were mainly taught sewing because most people believed that poor girls didn't need an education.

Sometimes, when they didn't have a teacher, Samuel Greg's sons and daughters taught the apprentices. Samuel hoped that he was preparing his apprentices for a lifetime of work at Quarry Bank. When they grew up, most of the apprentices chose to stay at the mill and some of the boys became well-paid clerks.

NO TIME TO RELAX

Sundays were supposed to be a day off for the apprentices, but there was very little time for them to relax. They had to walk two miles to church and then two miles back, once in the morning and then again in the evening. In church, they stood and listened to a very long sermon, and then there was Sunday School when they got back.

As well as being a place to rest their heads, the Apprentice House was also where the children attended lessons and where they could be seen by the mill doctor if they were ill or injured.

Then... ---> NOW!

Then and now

Can you count up the number of hours you spend in school? How does it compare with an apprentice's working day? And how do you spend your weekends and holidays? Imagine how amazed an apprentice would be to see all the leisure time you have now!

AN UNUSUAL PUNISHMENT

If apprentices working at mills across the country dared disobey their superintendent they were likely to be punished.

A common punishment used at the time was to make them hold a pair of wooden dumbbells with their arms stretched wide. This made their arms ache, but it also made them stronger to do their work...

Hold and stretch

You can try the apprentice punishment for yourself. Try holding a can of soup in each hand and stretch out your arms. Just try it for a moment and be careful not to hurt yourself!

WATCH OUT FOR FINES!

Workers had to pay some very large fines. If they were five minutes late to work, the fine was 12 pence, and if they were caught whistling they had to pay six pence. It would take six hours of extra work for an apprentice to pay off the fine for whistling!

WORKING OVERTIME

Even though the apprentices worked incredibly hard, they didn't get paid. The only way they could earn any money was to work extra hours at the end of their working day. Some apprentices had to work overtime to pay off fines. Others saved their money to treat themselves to a ribbon, a ruler or even a pair of shoes.

QUARRY BANK MILL.
RULES
AND
CONDITIONS OF EMPLOYMENT.

More work!

As well as working in the mill and doing their lessons, the apprentice boys had to work in the vegetable garden surrounding the Apprentice House. Gardening was hard work, but at least it was a break from the unhealthy atmosphere of the mill, and it provided some vegetables to add a little variety to the apprentices' diet.

BORING BUT HEALTHY

Imagine eating porridge for almost every meal! That was what the apprentices had to put up with. Every morning, after two hours' work, porridge was doled out to the apprentices. It was so solid it could be held in their hands. Lunchtime was the same. In the evening, MORE PORRIDGE, but cooked with vegetables. Twice a week there was stew – a small amount of meat cooked with lots of potatoes and vegetables.

Not porridge again!

Recipe

✋ Try mill porridge

1 Fill half a cup with porridge oats.

2 Then add just enough hot water to make the oats stick together in a lump.

3 Now try a mouthful. Don't add anything to make it taste better!

Smelly work!

Every week, the apprentice boys had to empty the contents of the privies, the outdoor toilets, and spread them all over the allotment. It was the smelliest job ever!

How did life in the mill affect the workers' health?

Cotton mills were desperately unhealthy places. All the rooms were kept very hot and damp, so the cotton could stay moist. The air was filled with cotton dust, and the giant machines made a deafening din.

AWFUL ACCIDENTS

Children were often injured while they were cleaning the machines. Others slipped and fell into moving machinery. Girls had to tie up their hair to stop it getting caught and ripped out and it was not unusual for a worker to lose a finger. Some workers, like Joseph Davenport, suffered very serious injuries. He caught his sleeve in a machine and his arm was ripped off. He died a few days later.

DREADFUL DISEASES

Inside the stuffy mill, diseases spread very rapidly. The cotton in the air clogged up the workers' lungs and irritated their eyes, and the constant noise of the machines meant that everyone suffered from headaches and deafness.

> Mills were very dangerous places. It was all too easy for fingers, clothes or hair to get caught up in a machine's moving parts.

CURIOUS CURES

When the workers fell ill, they were treated by the mill doctor. Some of his cures worked very well, but others seem very strange to us today. If you were a patient in the 18th century which of these treatments would you least like to have?

1 Blistering
Raising blisters on the skin. (This was believed to bring down a high temperature.)

2 Blood letting
Laying blood-sucking leeches on the skin. (This was a common treatment for any illness believed to be caused by too much blood in the body.)

3 Doses of foxglove tea
The foxglove flower produces a poison that stimulates the heart, but even very small doses can cause death. (Foxglove tea was generally given to people with swollen hands or feet. It cured the swelling, but it often killed them!)

Doctors used leeches to suck their patients' blood. Imagine how it felt to have a slimy, wriggly leech sucking at your arm!

The doctor would check every child who arrived at Quarry Bank to make sure they were fit for work.

Try mee-mawing

Because the mill was so noisy, the workers learned to lip-read. They moved their lips in an exaggerated way which they called 'mee-mawing'. You can try mee-mawing with a friend. Take turns at saying a sentence silently while your friend tries to understand it. See how far apart you can get and still be able to lip-read.

No time-wasting

The mill sheds were incredibly smelly. Instead of wasting time away from their machines, some of the male workers went to the toilet where they were stood – using a bucket!

Amazing machines

When Quarry Bank mill was built, it contained machines for preparing and spinning the cotton thread. Later, looms were introduced, for weaving the cotton thread into cloth. The giant machines at Quarry Bank were made from wood and iron. As they worked, they created clouds of cotton dust and made a deafening, thumping, creaking and clacking noise.

PREPARING THE THREAD FOR WEAVING

The bales of cotton that arrived at Quarry Bank mill were a mass of tangled fibres. They had to pass through several machines before they were ready for weaving. These machines included:

A scutcher
that broke down the fibres and removed any seeds and leaves

A carder
that brushed and cleaned the fibres

A finisher
that divided the cotton into thick strands of fibres, known as rovings, which were wound onto bobbins

A spinning mule
that drew out the rovings to the correct thickness and twisted them to make them into strong thread

A winding frame
that rewound the threads onto beams ready to be used on the weaving loom

You can still see a spinning mule at work in Quarry Bank.

LOOMS

Weaving looms have a set of threads, called the warp, stretched tightly across their frame, while a different thread, called the weft, is held in a shuttle and passed over and under the warp thread to make the cloth. At Quarry Bank, the process of raising and lowering the warp was done by giant wooden looms, which also sent the shuttle racing backwards and forwards.

WATER AND STEAM

At first, the mill's enormous water wheel provided all the power to drive the machines, but by the 1800s the wheel could no longer be relied upon. In 1810, the first steam engine was installed at Quarry Bank and water power was used along with steam.

Do your own weaving

You will need:

* A piece of stiff card, measuring roughly 15 cm by 25 cm
* Pencil
* Ruler
* Scissors
* Sticky tape
* Two balls of strong wool (contrasting colours look best)

1 Draw lines across your card 1 cm apart then use your scissors to make a cut of about 1 cm at both ends of each line.

2 Wind wool across the card to make your warp threads and fix the thread at the back of the card with sticky tape.

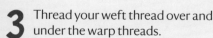

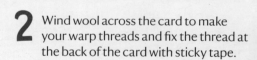

3 Thread your weft thread over and under the warp threads.

4 When your weaving is finished, cut through the warp threads at the back of the card. Then tie a knot at the end of each pair of threads.

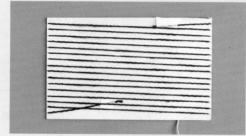

Industry takes off!

Quarry Bank was built at the start of a period of great change in Britain. This period is now called the Industrial Revolution and it lasted from around 1760 to 1840. During the Industrial Revolution, mills and factories were built, towns and cities grew rapidly, and a network of railways spread out across the country.

↑ NORTH & ↓ SOUTH

Change was much more rapid in the north of England than in the south, and Manchester and Liverpool grew especially fast. Many people travelled north to find jobs. Five families from southern England went to work at Quarry Bank and settled there for life.

The factory-filled city of Manchester was just 12 miles from Quarry Bank.

VICTORIAN TIMES

Queen Victoria reigned from 1837 to 1901.
In the Victorian period, Britain became known
as the powerhouse of the world.

During Queen Victoria's reign, Britain's factories
really took off. In this period, Quarry Bank mill
was run by Robert Hyde Greg, Samuel's second
son. Quarry Bank mill was very successful until
the 1870s, but then it began to lose business,
and the mill finally closed in 1959.

In the 19th century, some laws were passed to
make life better for workers in factories and mills.
Very young children were no longer allowed to
work in factories, and cages were built around the
machines. This cut down on accidents, but life
was still very hard for the workers.

Be an Industrial Revolution detective

Can you find a railway, mill or factory near you that
dates back to the time of the Industrial Revolution?
You could take some photos or make a drawing of it.

CHILDREN'S JOBS

If you were a poor Victorian child, you could
end up working in a mill, or you might work as
a chimney sweep's boy or be sent down a mine.

Victorian chimney sweeps forced young
boys to climb inside hot, crumbling chimneys
and push their brushes up towards the sky.
The boys were always covered in scrapes
and burns. Many of them suffered serious
accidents and some fell to their death.

Children working in mines pushed heavy
carts of coal through long, dark tunnels deep
underground. Very small children crouched
in the dark for hours, opening tunnel
doors to let the carts go through.
Which do you think would have
been worst: working in a mill, up a
chimney or down a mine?

Village life

For most people working at Quarry Bank, the village of Styal was home.

At first, most of the workers came from families living in the village. Later, Samuel Greg built cottages in Styal for his workers. Most workers' cottages housed a large family in the four rooms, and a single person or a couple without children in the cellar rooms. Each cottage had an outside toilet, known as a privy. The cottages were very crowded, but compared with the city slums, they were comfortable and healthy places to live.

This row of homes was built for the mill workers.

GROWING VEGETABLES

In front of each worker's cottage was a small strip of land, called an allotment, where people grew their own vegetables, such as cabbages, peas, beans and turnips. The Apprentice House also had a large garden for growing fruit and vegetables and herbs for medicines. This meant more work for the apprentices, but it added more variety to their diet.

A SHOP, A SCHOOL AND A CHAPEL

In the 1820s, the Gregs made some great improvements to village life. Samuel opened a village shop while Hannah Greg paid for a school for the village children. The Gregs also built a chapel in the village, but many people still made the long walk to church in the nearby town of Wilmslow.

Everything you need!

The village shop stocked everything the workers might need to live. As well as food, it stocked pots and pans, tools, brushes, furniture and clothes. People could buy everything they needed at the shop, so they rarely needed to leave the village.

Then and now

What kind of things do you spend your pocket money on? They're bound to be more exciting than the treats the apprentices saved up for. Records from the village shop show that clothes and ribbons were popular treats for the apprentices. One boy bought a dog's lead, even though the apprentices couldn't keep pets. Perhaps he liked to pretend that he had a little dog to be his friend?

The workers' cottages were better than the slums of Manchester but without running water, gas or electricity life would still have been hard.

Don't be late!

People in Styal village could hear the bell on the mill roof. The bell was rung to tell the workers when it was time to go to work, when it was time to take a break, and when the working day was over.

Gardens, woods and river

GRAND GARDENS

Hannah and Samuel Greg created a beautiful garden around Quarry Bank House. They even built a glasshouse, so that their gardeners could grow plants from distant lands. Grapes, melons and pineapples were served to guests at Quarry Bank House – quite a contrast to the workers' porridge!

Beyond the gardens were the Quarry Bank woods. The Greg children loved playing in the woods, and you can still explore them today.

SPOTTING WILDLIFE

Look out for animals and birds as you explore the grounds of Quarry Bank. If you're very lucky, you might spot a tree-creeper in the woods, a kingfisher on the river banks, or an otter in the river!

Spot the mini-beast

Can you find the mini-beasts shown here? Look for them in the grounds of Quarry Bank or in a garden or park near you.

Once you've found a mini-beast, put a tick beside it.

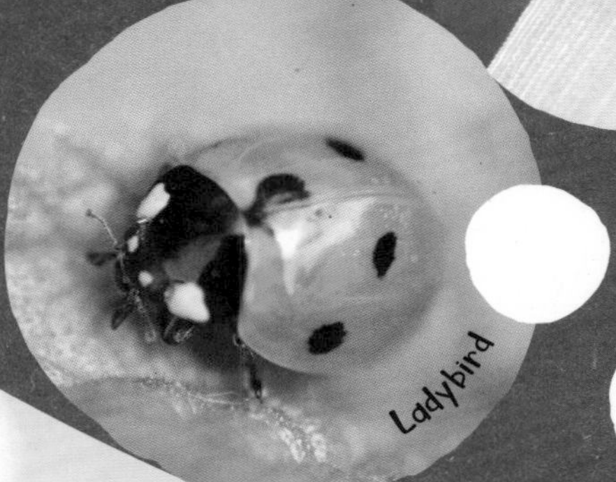

Centipede

Woodlouse

Beetle

Butterfly

Ladybird

Spider

FISH ON THE MOVE!

The River Bollin is home to salmon and trout. Recently, a fish pass has been built at Quarry Bank so they can swim upstream for the first time since 1800, when a weir was built across the river.

Robert's owl

The Greg's second oldest son, Robert, was fascinated by animals. He used to keep an owl in a cave by the river. You can still see the cave today.

Quiz

1
How many children did Samuel Greg have?

A 6
B 9
C 13
(p.3)

2
What kind of power was used at Quarry Bank?

A Water power
B Electricity
C Solar power
(p.3)

3
How many children lived in the Apprentice House?

A Fewer than 30
B More than 80
C Around 50
(p.3)

4
Where did the raw cotton come from?

A Australia
B Germany
C America
(p.3)

5
How much did children earn a week at Quarry Bank?

A 3 shillings (= £14)
B 1 pound
C 8 shillings (= £36)
(p.5)

6
What is kissing the shuttle?

A Sucking a thread through a hole in the shuttle
B Giving the shuttle a kiss for luck
C Touching the shuttle very lightly
(p.5)

7
What is doffing?

A Removing your hat before starting work
B Coughing quietly
C Removing full bobbins of thread
(p.5)

8
What did scavengers do?

A Look out for mice
B Crawl under machines to remove cotton fluff
C Search for food
(p.5)

9

What is 'slopping out'?

A Throwing away the remains of the porridge
B Washing up
C Emptying a chamber pot
(p.8)

10

How many miles did the apprentices have to walk on Sundays?

A 8 miles
B 4 miles
C 6 miles
(p.9)

11

What were the girls taught in their lessons?

A reading
B writing
C sewing
(p.8)

12

What is mee-mawing?

A Talking in an exaggerated way
B Making a noise like a mouse
C Asking for more porridge
(p.13)

13

What is a scutcher?

A A tool for scratching your back
B An apron worn by workers
C A machine to break down cotton fibres
(p.14)

14

Which food did the workers NOT grow in their gardens?

A Cabbages
B Pineapples
C Turnips
(p.20)

Answers

Page 5

1 D
2 A
3 E
4 C
5 B

Page 22

1 C
2 A
3 B
4 C
5 A
6 A
7 A
8 B
9 C
10 A
11 C
12 A
13 C
14 B